Elements of Chance

Also by Arthur J. Stewart:

Rough Ascension and Other Poems of Science
Bushido: The Virtues of Rei and Makoto
Circle, Turtle, Ashes
The Ghost in the Word
From Where We Came

Elements of Chance

poems

Arthur J. Stewart

CELTIC CAT PUBLISHING
Knoxville, Tennessee
2017

First edition copyright © 2017 Arthur J. Stewart. All rights reserved.

Elements of Chance: poems / Arthur J. Stewart

ISBN: 978-1-947020-03-0

Celtic Cat Publishing
Knoxville, Tennessee
CelticCatPublishing.com

We look forward to hearing from you. Please send comments about this book to the publisher at the address above. For information about special educational discounts and discounts for bulk purchases, please contact Celtic Cat Publishing.

Manufactured in the United States of America
Cover art by Justin A. Dickerman-Stewart
Library of Congress PCN: 2017949070

For Amit, and Tommy, and Lynn, and Chuck, and Rebecca, and Tony, and Mary, and Ian, and Mike, and John, and the hundreds and hundreds of other wonderful scientists I've had the pleasure of working with, one way or another, over the years.

Contents

Preface and Acknowledgments xi

Doing the Garden Plot by Mantis 3

Outside Comes Out 4

Balance 5

Elements of Chance 6

Sometimes It's Tough 11

Hardwired to Test 13

Heisenberg and Spooky Action at a Distance 14

Roots of Synchronicity 15

Stuck 17

Causalland 19

So What's Up 21

General Relativity 24

An Accounting 26

Another Crown 28

Casting Back 30

Old Textbooks 32

One Can Chronicle 33

The World Song 35

Doggie Dillon 36

The Damned Thing 38

Sandhill Cranes, Hiwassee Wildlife Refuge 40

Seen and Unseen 41

A Young Opossum in February 42

Atmospheric Phenomena 43

Firing up the Aurora Borealis 45

The Nazca Plate 46

Well Now, What's This? 47

Siberian Traps 48

North, Meet South 49

Edges 50

Errors by Eels 52

The Little Bones 54

DNA Methylation 55

We're Packed   56

A Weak Whisper   57

Wheel-Wheel-Horn   58

North and South   59

Up and Over   61

Transition to Summer   62

The Bunny Hour   63

The *H. L. Hunley*   65

Ever Which Way   67

Nanophotonics   68

Ice on the Koi Pond   70

Up Periscope   71

Command   72

Homes   73

Excess   74

Luck   76

Just One of Those Things   77

Eccentricity   78

What's Up 79

What's in a Word 81

How to Start a Poem 82

This Like That 83

Pushed Out, Drawn Up 85

Which by Definition Is 86

Facts in a Dream 87

No Chance 88

I Let Myself Move Down or Up 89

The Durability of Monet 90

Today I Am Rowing 91

This Far 92

About the Author 95

Notes 97

Preface and Acknowledgments

Poetry and science are not at odds with one another. Rather, these two great constructs support each other, arm in arm. So here we have it: *Elements of Chance*, my sixth book of science-flavored poems for scientists, focuses thematically on causality, the cornerstone of science.

Over the past thirty years, I've walked the fractal boundary of science and tried to communicate, through poetry as best I can along the way, what is in science, and what is out. This task has been challenging in part because science is by nature fluid and greedy: it grows constantly as it assimilates new information, coiling and curling, frothing at the soft edges of ambiguity. The task of communicating science through poetry has been challenging, too, because many scientists ignore poetry, and many poets, insofar as possible, avoid science.

Yet, science and poetry both depend upon our human abilities to meld data from five traditionally acknowledged senses—sight, hearing, taste, smell, and touch. The data-flow into our brains through these sensory pathways allows us to understand the world. If we see a hammer coming down forcefully to smash something on an anvil—a roasted peanut, for example—scientists and poets both know from related experience more or less what to expect. We can anticipate the sudden metallic and reverberating clang of hammer on anvil; we expect small fragments to fly; we can predict the nut will be converted to a lumpy, smeary bit of paste; and up close, after the fact, we can detect the peanut-butter smell and feel the oily texture, verifying our suppositions.

But our senses are very limited. The retinas of human eyes, for example, work well for radiation of wavelengths between about 400 and 700 nanometers, and wavelengths of light outside this range are largely invisible to us. Honeybees can see things we can't see; dogs can smell things most of us can't begin to smell. Bats can hear sounds at much higher pitches than we can hear, and Monarch butterflies are sensitive to the magnetic fields of the earth. Facts definitely matter, oh yes, they do—but we're human, too: we infer, we deduce, we suppose, and we guess a lot, both consciously and subconsciously.

Second by second, a huge fraction of our incoming sensory data-flow is processed by our brains subconsciously. It must be, or we'd be swamped and drowned in short order by the deluge of information—analogous to a denial-of-services attack in the hacking world. So the tic-toc of a clock fades into the background, until you pay attention to it. Then, suddenly, when you begin paying attention, it can be astonishingly loud.

Sometimes I think we are at risk of losing ourselves by putting too much confidence in what we think we know. And sometimes I think we may be at risk of losing ourselves, too, by frequently and incorrectly assigning effects to speculative causes through our dependence on subconscious processes: the ghost of a thing can be incorrectly identified as a shadow, or a bad outcome can be incorrectly interpreted as the result of a prior misdeed. The oh-so-narrow pathway of what truth is grays off into fog on both sides. Each step should feel like a precarious and precious thing. That's my deep wish for the world.

A quote from *The Lives of a Cell: Notes of a Biology Watcher* (Lewis Thomas, 1974) seems appropriate in introducing the reader to *Elements of Chance*: "There is a tendency for living things to join up, establish linkages, live inside each other, return to earlier arrangements, get along, whenever possible. This is the way of the world. ...It is a Chimera, a Griffon, a Sphinx, a Ganesha, a Peruvian god, a Ch'i-lin, an omen of good fortune, a wish for the world."

Grateful thanks to the editor of *Big Muddy: A Journal of the Mississippi River Valley*, where "Ever Which Way" first appeared. Thanks also to *The Hoosier Science Teacher*, where several poems in this collection were first published. None of the other poems in this collection have been published elsewhere.

Elements of Chance

Doing the Garden Plot by Mantis

It's just sludge-drudgery, at first—
using a Mantis to do the job
a righteous tiller should be doing: the little thing
roars like a bee and hops
from clod to clod, too light to settle deep.
Such a small tank, too, for the blended fuel,
a mixture of gas and oil sucked in to feed the two-

cycle engine. But slow as the sun proceeds
its arc and buries itself behind the pines, the task
rounds out, gains meaning. It becomes

a challenge, a thing I want to do. One more row,
and another, then one more
after that. I try to make the talons bite
a full four inches, churning dirt behind, down
with wild onions, their pallid bodies
heaved up to the light of day, down
with the dried surface layer of dirt, mixed in
by whirling tines almost a blur, the occasional
root-snag winding around the axle between the tines,
and online later I see it has a solid

worm-gear transmission and the tines spin
an incredible 240 revolutions per minute. Well, the worms
in the garden today come to know the force;
the mad bee throws them here and there. I'd miss them
if I could but there's not a snowball's chance
of that, and by the time the sun hits low my arms

are exhausted, too: the hands
tingle and the fingers
want to cramp.

Outside Comes Out

I begin puzzling, leaning back
in my office chair, peering out
over the manicured lawn. The men
with big walk-behind mowers are

doing it now, manu-
facturing short and even grass from tall un-
even grass, and they're doing it,
it seems, with gusto.

It's important to do
a thing with intent. But of the multi-
tude of things one can do,
what's the best way to chose

which thing to do? At work
I sell them my time
and a small part of my brain. What's
missing is balance—the grass

outside is too even.

BALANCE

                           until

No more than a gos-   Looking back, *ex post*
samer thread separates good   *facto*: when
action from bad action and   for example the cards
   often it is im-   have been played, the
    possible to tell   in-depth
  which action is the   time for *a priori*
     right action   consideration
                                    is over, no
                                                    period
                                                      on
                                                    purpose

                                                    :‖

ELEMENTS OF CHANCE

At first
it's innocuous—like
serendipity, but that word
is too long, too bouncy, it has
the ring of artsy-craftsy and that's

not where we want to be, not
now: consider the nuances, the am-
plifications, the consternations,
the turmoil and trumpets, the flowery

show of multidisciplinary indignation when some-
thing you're responsible for
goes wrong: when something
goes down instead of up, or left
when your plan called for right, and right
there, you hit the nut—expectations

dashed, the un-
expected pepper in the pot, something but
whoops, it did the other thing and now
   there
      you
         are,

the picker, by golly, want it
or not, holding the pepper's pecker,
the she sells sea shells on the sea shore problem
squared up, eye-
ball to eyeball, it

and you, so what now?
Well, it's back to the coin-flip,
the turn of the card,
the stale roll
of the dice, the zero-or-one

charge comprising the bit, and how many
bits to the byte and the inevitable
dinkle in the match-up of
complementary (almost) base-pairs and
the supposedly random

independent assortment of chromosomes if not
genes, yet now that idea too is totally befuddled
and next door to flummoxed by the problem
of epigenetic inheritance: the little rascals, bless

their beady eyes, can be turned off
by methylation and methylation
can be propagated across generations, and
the environment can drive methylation so, gosh,
there's Lamark, without the nasty word

being said. Thus,
we're near full circle
of confusion: replete with half-
baked confidence, get out there guys
  (and gals) and begin

plowing the field with the wooden plough,
I don't care if it's tough, that's the job
that needs doing and there it is: exactly
the vivid dream I had fifty years ago, standing
in the middle of a large field, the shafts

of the wooden plough, p-l-o-u-g-h, that word because
    it was
a long time ago and because
it had that meaning to me then and there
I was with the difficult job of

choice: do it, or not.
And when I did it, not looking back, red soil
turned up on one side and white soil
turned up on the other, beautifully cross-
pollinated by the action of plowing and that's

exactly
where
I
am
right
now

doing my damnedest each day to put
things on the left to the right and
things on the right to the left, I'd fly
if I could
or if I thought

it would help. Now
let's let things uncurl a bit: ease out, as if
spreading the wings and to get there I'll say first read
"Easter Morning": that poem shows perfectly how to break
from the here and now to the grander view—the great birds

soaring the air, perfectly how to stepwise step from the hum-
drum little fragments of our individual lives to the greater rise
and casual air of life unbound, or at least bound less, not much
is needed to make that boundless transition to a more
relaxed state of being, tied to

a casual yet still firm link, created by substituting,
for example, a chain for a rod or a bar, the material
in either case being good-quality steel, augmented with a trace of
nickel, cobalt, tungsten, vanadium, and carbon of course, and the material
overall designed and comprised of nano-sized grains

grading to more meso-sized grains, so the grain boundaries
properly distribute the forces
of stresses and strains, causing
or allowing or
con-

tributing to greater material ductility, anti-
fragility, resistance to fracture, increase in strength. Well,
the fly-boys in that area will have
their way with these terms I'm sure but I'm pretty sure
I've got the basics right. Let's

move on. Center on
that word 'properly' for a moment and hold it
to heart. The fracture or catastrophic
failure of a metal-sample under stress relates
      of necessity

to intent: the word could be re-
placed with more
uniformity
and by that I don't mean starched white
shirt with blue embroidered name

of the company you keep, note the reflexive
return to neighbor, proximity, locality,
close approximation to another thing and
there we are, blasted
back to what counts: in us and

outside us, the inevitable need for dif-
ferentiation, the long for the yin and yang,
the constant desire for
unexpected predictability and there's

a screen door fitted
with a tensioning spring, ready to

snap shut.

Sometimes It's Tough

Can't get a go going
so far today, so let's start
with the weather: it is dark
and cold outside and the miserable
thumb on the left hand still hurts despite
the twice-daily dose of naproxen,
a chemically strong relative
of Ibuprofen, a non-
steroidal anti-
inflammatory drug
and that stuff can mess up
the stomach, so get some food down
first and yet

it still hurts and that
   makes
      me
         cranky

despite the coffee dosed
with creamer and honey, enough
to drive a summer-active
Italian honeybee wild: she might have

flown back to the hive excited,
do a waggle-dance to point
the way of heaven to others. But no,
I'm not like that either: I don't
point much or point at all, I just aim
to lead and show, pulling by the nose

if need be and putting it
right there. How annoying
to have to carry on: this morning I worked
first through a poem about a dead hound
by James Wright, now dead himself,
and in the poem he

took it upon himself
to scatter the bones of the hound across a field,
tossing the skull like a ball
and it was not good: in fact,
near pointless, as far as I could see.

Not long thereafter, the thirteenth
of the thirteen ways
of looking at a blackbird
caught my fancy: I could relate

to "and it was going to snow." And to
"The blackbird sat
in the cedar-limbs." That's fine

compared to the reckless scattering
of a dead dog's bones. Rocking

back in the chair, I thought, yes, sometimes
it's tough
to get a good go going;
sometimes it's tough
to keep pretending
you know where you're going to go.

Hardwired to Test

What chance
do we have? We're hardwired to test
things that are fun-
damentally at odds with basic laws
of physics: we know things should fall

under the force of gravity
or roll downhill; solid things should not

pass through other solid things
unscathed. And there are deep-
seated ecological and evolutionary
constraints, as well—we're afraid

at least at first of snakes,
spiders, bats; birds are OK
if plucked and grilled,
roasted, souped, or baked,
the savory smell entices, the abstract

draws in the curious: most oils float
on water. This morning a hairy wood-
pecker clinging near the top
of our church's belfry pounded
repeatedly, the sound re-
verberated like mad and being
    in a cranky mood

for no good reason I had to say
to myself, right on, bird—
it's a beautiful day, give'm hell.

Heisenberg and Spooky Action at a Distance

Given two entangled particles, A and B, spawned
from one particle by doubling
the original particle's wavelength and
when A and B then are sent

separate ways, far off from one another,
each one somehow still knows

what the other is doing. Convert B
to a polarized wave, and A
    knows it, instantly, and converts itself
to the opposite: A and B are correlated.

The apparent
communication between the two particles
about what's what can be
instantaneous: faster than light.
But that's impossible, they say. It is

spooky action at a distance. And now
quantum locality has been linked
    to the famous
    (drum roll please)
Heisenberg uncertainty principle: that is,
    you can't know

a particle's position and its momentum
at the same time. And how did they
figure out this new connection?

By reframing the question
and thinking hard.

Roots of Synchronicity

Today I dig for the *unus mundus* in a hole
for a new Blackgold Sweet Cherry tree.
I pitch great heaps of dirt to the left and the right
first by spade but tearing

occasionally at roots and rocks with a heavy
mattock—hard labor,
pure and simple, my mind is focused
on each strike but at last

just when I'm starting to think
there's no hope, oh, it's gone, it's gone, it's
not gone: with one more strike, it appears,
something glistening, dark and moist,
like an ancient bone, peeking
from the dirt at the bottom of the hole.
Both ends of the thing are still buried, each end
affixed maybe to something else,

to cause, perhaps, or perhaps to chance. Sym-
bolic representations whirl in my brain:
Schopenhauer, a scarab beetle,
Einstein, Leibnitz, Jung, the great
self-reflecting living mirror of the universe.

The Trickster resonates like a big bronze bell;
he pivots on his own command. He offers
archetypes and myths, an unlit candle,
a burnt match, a coil of rope, some binder-twine,
a pry bar, a bent nail: what is affixed and what is not?
For a moment I am lost, as if at sea. I do not know
which way is up. What deep correlations
draw the psyche out?

With a wave of his hand, the un-
canny intrusion of the un-
expected pops into place, allowing
a peculiar happenstance,
a delicate display of deeper meaning,
allowing something that belongs
both here and there and carries
odd significance at multiple levels:
a cluster of anomalies, un-
accountable observations emerging
as unsettled discrepancies to what I thought
I knew. Trickster steps through

multiple dimensions, cracks and crevices,
fractures, fissures, a broken façade; he is

a master of transitions. Leave something
at the boundary and it will be replaced
with another thing. Synchronicity
cannot be tested; it does not
make itself available
for prediction or control so
again I think to myself, looking
now into the dead hole,
sure, even at this age, go ahead,
keep searching for the ox,
good luck.

Stuck

We seem stuck mostly with the what-ifs and the if-thens—
we're so much
less facile with the if-ands, probably because
it is more difficult, by some
multiplicative factor. And thinking thus
this morning, while swinging
the legs in a walk, one
alternating with the other, I saw

    —oh, what
did I see? One thing
was a small cloud
of insects whirling: several beetles, of course,
and a moth or two, individually
circling and bumping, drawn by the light
of an early morning streetlight on a high pole,
the top of which

    arched over

the sidewalk so my shadow
on the sidewalk, in the dark before dawn,
first was thrown back
behind me, growing shorter

    and shorter
with each

swinging step until I was
almost directly

under the light with the bugs above and then
it began

lengthening before me, growing longer
with each step.

Causalland

It's well into June now and, well,
it's still disappointing: I've had
no deep insights and no
great truths. Truth is,

in Causalland all's well
it seems, for through
time, tic still
makes
toc
.

A decay function is an ex-
ponential expression,
often set up some-
thing like
this
:

$N_{(t)} = N_0 e^{-\lambda t}$, where t of course is
time and N is the amount of
the thing in question at
t equals zero and at t
equals some time
later and λ is the
exponential
decay con-
stant and
e is the
natural
log
&

the point is, we all
run out at
some
rate
.

Tic.
Toc.

So What's Up

1.

So what's up
in Causalland today? It's a place
where each thing is
clearly caused by a another thing
through time: a crisp world, much more
than just a place, much more
than just a chunk of land because

Causalland includes
actions and re-
actions of interacting things and
here by things I mean
more than things alone—think hard,
for example, and you can cause
this thing or that
in Causalland. Yet given all these
pronouns it seems
so vague: so let's go
for a short ride with a few specifics.

2.

This morning I discovered
as I walked to work the sky
alight with new day and as I shifted
my gaze from near to far or left to right
I kept seeing
flick displays
of what might be

flocks of quick-flying blackbirds,
peripheral, up high, just above
my line of sight, winging hard,
higher still and to the right—
just eye floaters, I hope, distracting,
not causing
something more.

3.

By close of work day
the temperature was hot: a few clouds
had piled up and leaves
on the redbud trees were hanging limp and still.
But in Causalland
       at that same time
it's still crisp: it's tic,
       it's toc,
it's snappy, fresh and chill.

4.

Circle the curving inner edge
of a thermal draft, a rising doughnut
of heated air. At five hundred meters,
crank the neck

a little to the left, center the gaze on down and
       wow!
the world looks so different there.

5.

This morning in the willow oak in the backyard
a small murder of crows
began cawing it up. I checked
but saw no owl.

Just cawing, I think, or jawing: con-
fabulating on conjugating while con-
gregating
after breakfast, or just col-

lectively deciding
what thing next to do.

6.

Click. Tic.
Back. Bok.

General Relativity

A hundred years
the theory has passed hard tests and still we find
new applications. Mass,
energy, and curved spacetime
collectively validate
gravitational radiation, black holes, and cos-
mology; neutrinos and photons,
spewing from a supernova
in the Large Magellanic Cloud, arrive
here at Earth, our little home,
within hours of each other, showing
they move at different rates, in line
with differences in mass, and light

and neutrinos take the curved path
of space-time, making
the speed of light seem slow
as it flows
curvaceously across the galaxy from stars
differing in age. My head

spins now under the whirl of planets and
neutron stars; my pulse
picks up. What a delight

to know these things have worked
like this
for hundreds of thousands of years:
we stared

back then up at night from
sparking fire at cave-lip, astounded

by pinprick bits of starry light that fell.

An Accounting

Yesterday I gave a good accounting
of my knowledge based on questions
I asked my optometrist about the ad-
visability of YAG laser treatment
for eye floaters. He waffled a bit at first, un-
certain, but then helped track down
information on who might do the job
in Knoxville. Short answer: no one.
Well then, I thought, it's time

to enlarge the sphere of the query; truck out
to the hinterlands—Florida, West Virginia,
perhaps as close as Nashville
or the western distal end of Tennessee: Memphis,
riverboats and BBQ, fresh catfish
perfectly fried, pecan pie. Tennessee's

an odd state, you know, long and narrow
viewed west to east, crinkled
at each end because
each end is bounded
by a river. The wife and I are looking
forward so much now to vacation, a time

for getting out and changing
what we see, hear, and smell—the flood
of contract numbers on spreadsheets will be

behind me; in front, white blossoms
on the turned-up tips of the sturdy arms of saguaros,
the end-of-summer smoke from a fire surging
a pine forest in northern Arizona,
the pungent smell
of just-wet greasewood, the surprising

snowballs of cotton bursting from sharp-
fingered fists on tens of thousands of plants
on thousands of acres of death-flat fields,
the astounding

leap from the runway by the jet as we
set off on adventure.

Another Crown

Phase I occurs after the needle-prick
puts in Novocain: then
the rubbery stuff goes in to make
an impression of the offending tooth.
Next the terrible shriek
of the drill begins. It runs

up the tooth and through the roots,
into the jawbone and up
into the tiny bones of the ear.
It goes

with the acrid smell-taste of tooth dust,
the spraying and sucking out
of the blood-salty water; repeatedly
I tell the physical self to relax:

      un-tense

the muscles of neck, shoulders, arms
as he keeps saying

now open.
Now close.
Now open again.

Then he packs the gumline
around the tooth with something
like an absorbent piece of string pushed deep
and in goes a different minty
rubbery stuff which
after a few minutes firms to hold
the shape of the tooth that's been
drilled down. Now close.

Now open again.
Now close.
Now open again. The temporary

cap goes in at last, the numbed
jowl trembles
by itself.

Casting Back

A poem should reverberate and resonate
from simple harmonics and more comp-
licated and nuanced points—here's an example
set in an Arizona desert: me,

alert to the slender body of a whip-
tail lizard, known then as *Cnemidphorous*,
      of which
there are many species, including *tigris*, yet see

it is so easy to digress and it, the lizard,
moves almost constantly, creeping forward
now a little, or pausing briefly before moving again
from greasewood shade to sun to

dappled shade, over and around small stones,
while I, large and clunky by contrast,
take a step and pause, and take a step
and pause, the right arm

out straight holding the radio aerial salvaged
from a junked car and it, the aerial, being
extended fully, and to its tremble-tip is affixed
a foot-long piece of waxed string with a noose on the end that,

if one is lucky, tenacious, and careful, can be slipped
gently over the lizard's head, thus
snaring the creature.

    But what then?

A close inspection of the delicate claws, the little plate
of the ear behind and slightly lower than the eye,
the smooth snugged-up scales
on the head and beneath the jaw, tiny beaded scales

on the back, more snake-like scales
on the belly, and coarser scales on the long tail
starting just distal to the flanged-out
alligatorish pair of rear legs.

Whiptails are difficult to noose, being
just leery enough to keep moving,
moving, moving. But if caught—
they lose, I win: just close inspection, then

set free. Easy
peasy. So here
I also pause, and invite you, the reader
to cast back, too:

take a moment. Stop
moving. What's your game, what
are the rules and
where do you want to be?

Old Textbooks

Nothing at all at first.
No feather fluff, no hawk beak, not even a quick
onion, pepper, squash, or leek. I sit. The sun
works over the eastern ridge, steady and slow;
the long shadows of trees
in the yard grow shorter, slowly.
The calico cat
we call Hannah sits on a pile of books
at my upstairs office window, looking out. And
speaking of books, and speaking of
looking out:

Yesterday I took a full box of old textbooks
from college classes I had 40 years ago
to the high school and dropped them off.
Some are still good. Parasitology, for example,
has advanced a lot
in terms of molecular this and that but
a tapeworm is still a tapeworm, with a life cycle,
and the life history

of the fence lizard, *Uta stansburiana*, has not changed much
despite global climate change, urbanization, speeding up
of the hydrological cycle, or habitat
fragmentation. Some young student

might yet learn a little, might
do good things in the world, blow off
the dust, get
interested
perhaps
by accident.

One Can Chronicle

One can chronicle
the aches and pains
of growing old—I feel,
for example, a stenosis coming on

near the proximal end of the
esophagus, perhaps associated with the
lower esophageal sphincter; then there's the

arthritic left thumb, and the plantar fasciitis
of the left foot, and the large increase
in eye floaters (those bastards
are so distracting), and the
cataracts continue to get worse and the

wheeziness that accompanies
any strenuous work and let's get past that crap

to the good stuff. Last night
we went to dinner, took the daughter out
for her birthday and a dozen
others were there, too, and
      we had such good fun

chatting, me not poking too much
fun at the ex and she
staying away from weird conspiracy theories
for a while, starting the event

with French fries loaded—drizzled
with melted cheddar cheese and
bits of real bacon, not bacon bits,
and a big birthday card,

signed by everyone
documenting
presence, life, enjoyment,
a good time.

THE WORLD SONG

When our daughter was three or four years old
snug on the back seat of the deep blue
Honda Civic, she would sometimes sing

what she called the World Song. This song
started softly with the words
"The world is beautiful and great,"
and her voice

was beautiful, too, and almost every time
the song went on for a long time,
touching

this part of the world, then another,
differing somewhat with each singing
in details because,
she said, when asked,

the world is constantly changing.
And that answer was beautiful, too, and truth
reverberates still in her song.

Years later I'm driving
to work on the bridge over the Clinch River;
the river is dark, the moon a sliver, I think

we might all
awake with this morning's light
and sing at least the first few lines.

Doggie Dillon

Our dog Dillon had a little
carcinoma between two toes
on the left front paw and
it was malignant and we had them
take it off but
they couldn't get it all because
of where it was and
without radiation treatment to follow
his chances were not good. So

he went through that, too: 17
treatments and to keep him
from licking the raw meat
when the skin sloughed off

      he became
a cone-head: we slipped
the diabolical plastic cone
over his grizzled head and lashed it
to his collar. For weeks it was

terrible to see him
learn to swing the thing
this way and that as he
navigated chairs, table legs,
door frames, the edges
of bookcases and

when going outside we put a bootie
on his tender foot to protect it
from wetness—dew

on the fresh grass, and
he got used to that, too—learned to raise

the foot up so we could slip the bootie on
before we let him out. Weeks later
it was amazing to see him

swinging the cone this way and that as he
plunged his way
doggedly through weeds, snaring it

on this thing or that before
jerking it free, again and again, he was
so determined
to be happy, alive.

THE DAMNED THING

When the damned thing came back
after radiation, we knew
it was a problem.
Chemo, the last hope

with Dillon-dog swallowing
yellow pills and dragging thereafter
for days of diarrhea and lethargy
even as the soft lumps grew bigger
and the whites of his eyes

grew brown. Finally

his gaunt frame, the one
that once held
his burley body up, could not
take more. He curled

on the floor, his ribs
prominent as masts holding limp sails,
and through that bad night his breathing

grew more labored; he became
something different than he was: he became

Dillon, working for his life,
the hardest race he ever ran,
the breathing
in and out, in and out, the rhythm

sometimes spot-checked with a cough,

and as the sun rose that morning we called
the hospice vet to put him down.
That part, at least, was easy.

Sandhill Cranes, Hiwassee Wildlife Refuge

In a great voice, a vast group rises,
many hundreds, creaking and croaking
distinctive rattle-calls like frogs, and they circle
as a flock the arc of the land: mudflats
in the foreground, shallow water behind that,
and the thick body of the river behind that,
and a forest behind that,
and fog behind that, and far off
a range of mountains rising above the fog.

It is winter and thus austere.
The sun is rising behind us.
Frost covers the dead grass in shaded places,
but it is gone on the dead grass in the little places
where the sun has reached.

A man's voice
floats from among the people watching
the flock: they'll be gone,
all except the old and lame, by about
mid-March, when their food
is exhausted.

I look left then right: hundreds of acres
of corn-stover stubble-fields
where the birds work when they land.

They do not seem to worry
in the least about mid-March.
Instead, they take their time
working the fields, bending gray necks, a distinctive
bright red patch on the crest of each head.

Seen and Unseen

Six a.m. and I'm crossing
the beautiful Clinch River by bridge,
driving to work

       but I can't see

the river's slow beauty beneath me: it is too dark—
the moon is thin, so the best I can do
is remember. I note to myself:

       there's beauty

in the world, seen and unseen. It can be seen
in the way a satin-black horse bends its muscular neck
to the grass; it can be seen

       in the way the black water works

by gravity in a river, along the banks on each side
where snags and rocks touch it,
pull it into motion.

A Young Opossum in February

It's always the note after the note, rising
or falling in pitch, louder or softer, starting
abruptly or slowly—the note
after the note of now. In this brief
analysis of life I find
myself, the peephole of me, looking out
to no avail. Driving
home last week after work it was

dusk near dark. It had been
a warm day, the first one in a while; the snow
was retreating in rough patches here and there
and I saw crossing the road quick
for an opossum, a young opossum: on delicate
tiptoes, the creature's little legs moved fast
but the overall rate
of progression of the small gray body

was not great, causing my smile.

Atmospheric Phenomena

Here and there, haboobs—intense
dust storms: in the Sahara desert,
across the Arabian Peninsula, throughout
Kuwait, and in deserts
of Central Australia, the hot arid
and semiarid regions of North America

       and in the heart, especially

deserts in Arizona. Strong winds move in
from all directions, supporting
thunderstorm formation,
and when such storms collapse

       in despair winds rush out

       in all directions, particularly

in the direction of the storm's
forward motion and these winds,
in gushing, pick up
silt, dust, and dusty memories:
they approach
with little warning.

And virga, an observable

shaft of precipitation falling but which
evaporates or sublimes
before reaching the ground. The evaporation
cools the rushing air and accelerates it

       well beyond the self.

Not the same
as a dust devil whirled up: a
localized vertically oriented ro-
tating column of wind
driven by extreme

differences in temperature between
near-surface air and
the higher atmosphere. And of course

    St. Elmo's fire:

ionization of air molecules, a plasma,
a thousand volts or more
per centimeter with discharge being
especially intense at the ends
of sharp objects, the tips
of cattle horns,

dilemmas.

Unsteady
   weather, un-
steady emotions,
a ship
with storm-ragged sails, masts

      pointed with a blue flame—

Corpus sancti, oh holy body appearing
when the worst is past.

Firing up the Aurora Borealis

Many things start
at the edges of things, it's a
well-known fact and fact
of the matter is
if a thing starts
it tends to start
at an edge and move in.

Think, for example:
a flame eats
the end of a dry broken stick and lets loose
heat and light. And like that,
the aurora borealis is caused

by charged particles inter-
acting with the solar wind
high in the earth's magnetosphere:
      eating, eating
in line with the direction of the local

magnetic field, releasing
green-red sheets, curling
curtains of light.

The Nazca Plate

Buried in the little crook
of the west coast of South America,

where Peru
touches Chile, dia-

bolical ancient folds
get tense, get ready

to snap again: thrust-
faulting at a shallow depth—

a place
famous for big ones.

The Nazca plate is poised
to slide under the South America plate;

the oceanic crust and the lithosphere
of the Nazca plate begins

descending into the mantle beneath
South America and arches

its back; it pushes up
the Andes Mountains; they are

ragged snow-capped and serene;
up that high, the cold air

is thin yet carries an unheard sound,
a trembling ionospheric perturbation.

Well Now, What's This?

It's like the possibility of predicting
earthquakes from electromagnetic anomalies
in the ionosphere: the mechanism
is uncertain. Ions from deep
pressure-stressed rocks, perhaps, cause
mysterious glows
reported before the shaking starts,
and the resulting changes
in the abundance of positive ions also could account
for the odd

pre-earthquake behaviors of wild animals.
But things, you know,
get entangled at the edge of science—facts
and suppositions, un-
structured anecdotal reports get mixed with data
from well-structured monitoring networks
of tilt-meters and undersea transducers,
and classification errors
associated with remote-sensing
image analysis are non-trivial. The gray-

bearded guy studies the screen; he nods,
he scratches
his right ear with his left hand.

SIBERIAN TRAPS

The optometrist I saw today classified
degrees of lens opacity as
could, should, or must repair and
I first supposed and then I learned I'm good

for now: a mere con-
sequence of age, he said: I could
but not yet should, so I read

about the mass extinction of oceanic life
252 million years ago
at the Permian-Triassic boundary.
They think it was caused

by the Siberian Traps, a monstrous
volcanic eruption that released
3 million cubic kilometers
of basaltic lava and vast amounts
of carbon dioxide, methane and sulfur-gas

and that then caused,

by oceanic acidification, through
a reasonable chain of events,
The Great Dying.

North, Meet South

Camels, peccaries, bear dogs,
giant sloths, and terror birds lined up
ready to help
south meet north, north meet south,
at the Isthmus of Panama

15 million years ago, when
the land bridge first appeared.

But I had to look up
bear dogs: creatures classified
as members
of the now-extinct family Amphicyonidae
        evolving
from wolf-like to bear-like;
obligate carnivores coming over

to North America from Eurasia
by the trans-Beringian route and
coming up, south to north,

by the Panama isthmus,
and I think

        what a

funny word, and how odd
they walked,
digitigrade,
on the tips of their toes.

Edges

1. Functional

Most things start at an edge and move in.

    (the center cannot hold)

Think of a flame: it eats
the broken end of a dry stick and releases
energy as light and heat.

Think of the aurora borealis,
created by charged particles and the solar wind;
it aligns
with the local magnetic field and releases
energy in wavering
green-red curtains of light.

2. Dangerous

One slip
of a razor sliding
down the left wrist, the delicate edge where the skin
scarcely covers thin
pencils of blue.

3. Example

Ecotones are edges, places
where two kinds of habitats
come together: the habitats
exchange things. A forest
abutting a grassland, or the place
where a grassland snugs to a desert.

4. Situational

I walk at the edge
of poetry and science; I live
day by day on an edge.

Errors by Eels

It's like
when I try to spell calendar,
or archaeological anthropology—I find
opportunities for errors. Yet beyond error,
I was pleased today to learn at last
they're fishing for information
on the migratory patterns of the American eel:
these slippery fish slither
downstream in freshwater rivers on the east coast of the U.S.

and then seem to disappear
yet somehow their babies end up
in the Sargasso Sea. Not long ago, 33 adult eels were tagged
with small tracking devices, and 28 of the eels
later surfaced at sea
and the devices they carried broadcast

data like mad on water temperature, salinity, and
eel location. Six of the eels were tracked
for more than a month. First, they scooted north
along the Continental Shelf, sampling
water temperature and salinity before

    detecting something—some

combination of subtle factors, perhaps—
the moon, the stars, even the hint
of a scent of a long-lost memory. And then

    they broke free,

aiming hard south toward the Sargasso, swimming
near the surface of the sea at night, and much deeper by day.

Of the original 33, more room
for chance and error. Several
may have been eaten by predators;
some might have starved; and some,

it seems, just disappeared.

The Little Bones

The little bones in the hands
tell a story—the squeeze-grip
physics of holding tools
and making flints. We came
down from trees, giving up
an arboreal mode of life. They say

pollical distal phalanx
asymmetrical metacarpal heads
proximodistally oriented joint
configuration and then

something I can read, a thumb-
to-finger ratio. We came,
I figure, from such
and such and changed
through time, learning

at last to flip off
the bad driver coming up
too fast behind you at the stop sign.

DNA Methylation

We wonder
    whether, how, and when
        methylation happens, turning off
           the activities of genes: the scaffolding
    sequence of our genes is fixed, of
  course, but their activities
differ from
tissue
    to
tissue,
    through time,
  so all we are
 is determined by those
  little methyl groups,
  it's like hardware
        and soft-
           ware,
              or
                a piano:
              the keys are fixed,
                it's how you play'em,
      bud.

We're Packed

with mobile parasitic DNA mobile elements;
most of these
are non-functional remnants; a few

are still active
and can jump about,
causing genetic mischief, and

hair follicles practice
quorum sensing, at least
in mice, and

octopuses can move
their heads and eight arms
independently, in-

dicating
a sophisticated central command
generator in the motor center

of their brains, a
propensity of density! Thick
sequences of fossil-rich marine sediments

tell us with great confidence
we're headed for trouble.

A Weak Whisper

Two scientists built an algorithm to extract information on time from noisy data with corrupt time stamps. Think of it as restoring the initial sequence of a deck of cards after it has been shuffled.

"There are some remnants of the original sequence information in the shuffled deck," said the senior scientist. "There's a weak

      whisper of time, like a faint voice in a loud party."

They conceived the algorithm while working with data from a project tracking the movements of molecules using an X-ray free-electron laser. Slow   it   down.

An X-ray free-electron laser uses an ultra-quick flash of light to grab a "snapshot" with such speed that the sequence of snapshots yields a slow-motion movie of extremely rapid events.

   You need

hundreds of thousands of snapshots, plus knowledge of the precise time when each snapshot was taken. The scientists used their algorithm to reconstruct a clear movie of molecules as the bonds holding their atoms together were

              torn apart.

The algorithm resolves time, identifies internal correlations to make sense of the ocean of snapshots; it could be used

      in cases where dynamic histories are poorly known—geology, metrology, chemistry, biology, and astronomy—

a treasure trove of possible applications.

WHEEL-WHEEL-HORN

In this crazy world

now they've discovered
a protein, Rqc2, involved with

protein synthesis. Turns out, it's not just
ribosomes and messenger RNA alone at work, manu-

facturing useful things. But
Rqc2 is not great

at the job. It's like
a factory metaphor, an assembly line

extended. The smart hands
went home early so a half-programmed robot

continues the job, but
not well. It's like

trying to make an automobile by sticking on
two repetitive pieces only: a horn,

a wheel, another wheel, a horn, a horn,
randomly, a wheel, two more horns,

what do you get? A
wheel-horn-horn-horn-wheel-horn—

you can't possibly drive it
off the lot.

North and South

1.

North is Seamus Heaney:
all about the pitch and yaw of self against
the path one takes
over slabby layers of stone laid down and

fractured through time by gnarly root—
heather, bogbean, downy oat-grass,
green-ribbed sedge, a long
list of plants

whose growth is driven by wispy sun
and wind and ice and heat; each one is
dedicated to pressing
its lovely self between before

abruptly forcing up
a bit of rock, a crumb
of black-rot soil, centering
now on the voice of home. Thrice round

the old dog turns
slow and stiff; he sniffs
the bed-site—his habit
before settling down.

2.

South is a slow gumbo:
okras, tomatoes, celery, bell pepper, onion,
Cajun spices, seafood, on rice

and here, on a clear day
from our small back deck,
the Appalachian Mountains. Yes,
they're smoky: a sultry

terpene-fostered haze
delicate as morning fog on fern and
close by, now in the leather-leaf,
having flitted there from the holly

and before that,
from the bursting dogwood,
a Carolina wren: this old dog

tilts his nose and sniffs
the pollen-laden air; he turns
to the deck and finds a chair.

Up and Over

Charleston, South Carolina—a place
where they know
rice, indigo, and wrought iron, thick
mortar, brick arches, crabs and shrimp,
oysters and fish: the place oozes

sweet honey of Civil War history,
gray and blue, muskets and cannon,
multiple flags.

So many three-story houses
are stripped to their original
ornamentation: wavy window glass,

earthquake bolts
stubbed tight, wood floors,
haint blue porch ceilings. On a harbor tour
chugging toward Fort Sumter, the water

ripples by breeze, glints
from the back of the occasional porpoise
arching to air, re-
entering the world of water.

Transition to Summer

In *Glare*, the poet Archie Ammons shined
his copper pots and pans; he hung
his words out there, stubby rafts
crafted of gnarly hoodwinked lines.
What are we to make of such?
For one, they ready me to fire up and off,

a bottle-rocket this sudden time of year—
just scratch the match and touch it

to the fuse: this is,
       after all,
just a warmup to the blander
blue blanket of summer: lay it
on the new-mown grass; the fire-

flies are hanging around, total dead-
beats in terms of large movements
but beating their little wings
like mad in the cooling air and

out there, in the neighborhood
someone is grilling: the char-
coal-blasted de-
licious odor of burgers makes me want a beer.

The Bunny Hour

In early evening we place ourselves
in lawn chairs on the low deck
behind the house, overlooking
the large field beyond the grapevines, beyond

blackberry bushes, beyond the garden—
squash of three types, and okra plants,
and tomatoes, and two kinds

of melons, and spinach, and several of last year's
leftover lettuces, and one leggy bunch
of cilantros, and several other things
I've forgotten

and as we settle
from events of the day and from
the dissipating heat, we can hear
cicadas and from the pond, the occasional frog's voice

chugging through the upright stems of pickerel weed,
and the soft spill of water, and a lone tree frog, and the long
shadow of trees across the western half of the field

grows slowly: it's the only
sharp thing, and it is now

almost halfway across the sunlit field—
the bunny hour.

Two cottontails come out
from the forested area on the far side
and begin to play; one of them leaps,
kicking its heels up

in what seems to be exuberance, the other
more demure. They come
onto the sunlit part of the field
to play there, and sometimes in the shade;

and we enjoy each other's company.
As she talks about what happened
today I rub the calves of her slender legs,

and work her feet with my thumbs. The bold red
toenail polish is starting to wear
again; a chip gone there, and a thin line
of new nail-growth shows at the base of a toe;

each small thing
has significance. This evening
we consider a move. Should we
find or have built

a smaller house? With a sunroom,
and a writing room, and larger closets, perhaps
a screened-in porch overlooking
not a field like the field we look on here, but

closer to things: close enough
we might walk to a store
or to a café; we might
do that together and hold hands.

The *H. L. Hunley*

The *H. L. Hunley* sank three times, killing
in succession, five, eight, and eight
brave men cloistered
in her confines. Of eight

on a full crew, seven were there
to crank the screw and one
to navigate. She had arrived
earlier in Charleston by rail.

Upon successfully attacking
the USS *Housatonic*, she
survived an hour, gave a
blue-light signal for success and then

disappeared.

2.

In 1995, she was found
buried under silt, resting
on her starboard side, listing
at a 45-degree angle, en-

crusted with rust, sand, bits
of sea shells. She was raised
on August 8, 2000. Dixon, Collins, Ridgaway,
Wicks, Becker, Carlsen, Lumpkin, Miller

died at their stations: they were not
trying to escape when she went down
the third time. An inscribed 20-dollar gold piece
that had protected Dixon at Shiloh

was found, as well—this time a not so lucky
lucky charm.

3.

One can't afford to get too
filly-sophicle about little things like luck:
odd things pop up
like Bantam eggs, golf-ball-sized
speckled barnyard tokens of chance;
but so do fresh

road apples; cow pucky, bull
corn, you can work on down the list
to UFOs.

4.

And yet
I waffle:
with luck
it might be so.

Ever Which Way

Last Saturday at a Civil War reenactment event
just outside our little town, a woman
stood at the window of a food truck where several
had lined up to make purchase: she asked
the vendor some details
of purchase possibility, which her husband, in
Confederate gray, out of line and some

distance from the truck, wanted to know; so she
began relaying

questions from her husband to the vendor
and answers from the vendor to her husband,
turning her head on a swivel
and in a loud voice: Kin I get fries? Yes
to the fries. Buns have seeds? Yes, sesame, or no
if you want. What comes
with the nachos—kin I get
peppers, chili, onions? Yes, you can get'em

ever which way. The communication
was beautiful to me. The day
was special, too; the grass
was damp from last night's drizzle-rain; the trees
here and there were shaping themselves
toward gold and red, the sun
beginning to burn away the morning fog

    and there we were,

in gray or blue, not a lick
of science to puzzle at, just
pleasant talk
with each other, ever which way.

Nanophotonics

In *Science* before you know it you're down
into the nanoscale and femtosecond ranges;
they're discussing
bandgaps, phonons, metal-
dialelectric interfaces, wave-
guides, plasmon resonance and

thank goodness, something
I almost understand, simple
harmonic frequencies. I learn

the Purcell factor
is the spontaneous emission rate increase
due to enhanced photon mode density
in an antenna's optical near field
      whatever that means
it's a density of information, that's
for sure. Now how

to apply it? I sip my coffee and flip
the page to consider practical applications: read
medical diagnostics, molecular sensing,
surface-enhanced Raman spectroscopy,
DNA sequencing,
LEDs and photovoltaics,
metal nanowire networks, and
molecular quantum optomechanics

and when at last I give up and go
outside to the koi pond there's
a green frog, *Rana clamitans*, on a lily pad; he's
motionless in the sun;
        he makes
a sound like a banjo: short and loud, a set of re-
verberating "clungs."

Ice on the Koi Pond

Hard ice
on the pond this morning;
the white, orange, and black
koi are motionless

inches under the ice.
A bluebird alights at the pond's edge,
searching for surface liquid water.
There seems to be none

except that which is
beneath the ice
but then, tight around the dead stems
of remnant lizard's tail and

pickerel weed—a crevice
where water seeps up
when the beak goes in.

Up Periscope

Now and again
    slip-
ing through the dark
waters, one should pause, call stop

to the great engine and say
    to the engineer,
up periscope. From the dark
waters, up-slip-

ing with bubbles, the tube
where light then flows
more than 14 meters
from above to down, press

eyes to the ocular's steel shell: adjust
the focus, let come.

Command

You could roll
a pair of twenty-sided dice and turn
a number up to work with, or spin
the needle on a dial, or count
petals as you tear them
one by one from a daisy's head. But
the eeny meenie miny mo thing
is no good: it is
numerically so constrained—the odds
are set before you start so
how should we best fit

the day-by-day decision-needs of our
nubby little lives into
doing what we need to do? I make
chicken soup for lunch and do
the laundry after sorting lights from darks;
I spangle out at times unanswerable
questions to the universe. On a good day
it's good
to feel the cool slip
of water along the submersed hull and feel
the caress of micro-bubbles, the almost-silent

vibratory hum of the great engine: the one
that drives you, the one that drives
the urge to give and act on
the up-periscope command.

Homes

Sometimes great effort is devoted
to knocking out noise
of every type—the little jiggles
of sound, tiny spikes
in electrical transmissions, mag-
netic fields, stray neutrons, muons—

      little things
out of place. It can happen

when there's need to scrutinize
something with a fine-toothed comb. Next door

to a working pine forest
in the flatlands of Louisiana is home

to the ultra-sensitive
Laser Interferometer Gravitational-Wave Observatory
set to detect

ripples in space and time
caused when neutron stars or
black holes merge and also
not so far from
  the maybe-what-was

      last known home

of the beautiful
ivory-billed woodpecker,
Lord God Bird
   with no
period
  here
     on purpose

Excess

In the world of excess, too much
is a good thing and much too much
is better—three times a touch
is better than one, and five glorious roses
offer more beauty than one: in that world

even nothing is something
and an exuberance of anything
by more than one exceeds by far
a wondrous one. Yesterday

as the day slipped to late afternoon
the sun was a red ball aligned perfectly
to eye-level driving west, so we took

     some time to shop
at an Asian grocery in Knoxville, marveling
at the diversity of colors, items, smells.
Shrimp and fish, fresh or dried or salted or pickled,
bamboo shoots, palm hearts, many kinds of noodles,
a hundred sauces, flavors, tofu this and that,
brightly labeled cans, bottles and bags on shelves
and some things just out there
in gaping bushel baskets, or on tables or in bins:
pigs' ears, jackfruit, grapeseed oil, every aisle
an astounding festivity of color. Could this be an example,
I wondered, of poetic excess? We bought

a few small things—two types of ginger in jars, one
sliced for sushi, one pickled; a tin of jackfruit
and two kinds of soy sauce; we bypassed
the duck eggs and the delicately speckled quail eggs,

they'd not hatch in any case, and picked up
two packs of rice cakes with bean sauce,
kouhaku mochi, just to try them. The sun

by then had moved a little, or we had moved
          a little,
just enough, it was perfect.

Luck

Luck is
one side of chance, a two-sided
gold doubloon, air-spinning, sun-
twinkling. When it lands

we are happy or dismayed.

When it lands
the little brain
within the bigger brain
takes one step back.

Just One of Those Things

Once
or twice a year, some-
thing happens

with our shower water: turn it on, let it run
hot and suddenly it burps
a black-water pulse, a copper sulfide-laden

belch from the bowels of the 30-gallon aux-
iliary electric water heater
beneath the floor in the dark spider-

infested crawl-
space under the house.

Eccentricity

Odd, from the Old Norse word *oddi*:
meaning a point of land, something

that sticks out. Lop-
sided, off-
center. Out
of the ordinary, and it is

amazing how the human eye and brain
revel in small discrepancies.

What's Up

When walking up the driveway this morning
to fetch the Sunday paper, I found evidence
of a break in the water line under the road—a bubbling up
of water, flowing in the small channel caused

by the way the asphalt surface of the road
dipped a little at the road's edge
to meet the curb, and the water

was clear and running free
just like a small spring

although the system lacked
cress and well-smoothed stones,
and this small spring contained
no snails, of course: rather,
this water would instead, if tasted, taste

of chlorine and would have, if analyzed,
a characteristic city-water ionic signature
of sodium, potassium, calcium, and magnesium
balanced by a specific set
of anions, such as chloride, bicarbonate, phosphate
and so forth.

I'm quite sure about these things and yet

one can wonder
every time you see a bubble-up
of water from underground, it's like

McElligot's pool,
what's
really connected to what,
what's up
down there.

What's in a Word

Some words are so close
based on letters, syllables—un-
conventional, observational, unite,
untie: what's
the difference? The cosmic

microwave background still jiggles
from its ancient source, dusty
as an old pillow and optimistically
they're securing polarization data

at five frequencies to sort it out.

How to Start a Poem

In Word, go to full-screen view; set
initial conditions—font 12, Times Roman; type
a few words to get
the juices flowing, the fingers
limbered up, the blood moving
from the lungs (by way of
the pulmonary vein), to the brain
(by way of
the muscular aorta and its attending
carotid arteries).

Take a long, slow sip
of coffee, hot with cream and open
a random book of poetry—best if
it's good: it's hard to go wrong
with William Carlos Williams,

he could trace blood flow and oxygen
this way and that through the body
like no tomorrow and still make
astounding external observations
scrupulous in fact and most
admirable in detail, such as
the young sycamore
(and here I quote)

eccentric knotted
twigs

bending forward
hornlike at the top.

This Like That

William Carlos Williams wrote: "by the road
to the contagious hospital"—that's how he started
"Spring and All" and I

could start this like that,
or differently: let's try differently
just to be different.

In spring and all, we shoot past
images of mottled clouds, who cares they change so fast,
we could look for more durable signs, perhaps

the shaggy-barked sycamore: it is so large
two large men can't reach around it
holding hands and in spring it creaks

under the rhythmic pulse
of rising sap; its heavy roots groan
as they seek, find, capture, and bring up

water, nitrate, calcium, iron,
core constituents for making
chlorophyll, so much

sparkling new in spring, at first
not even anthocyanins and xanthophylls, pro-
tective pigments,

chemicals
sun-driven and sharp to the mind and eye and there,
I find unburying itself

from winter's wet
dead leaves at the base of the sycamore,
a toad, body still cold and warty: he has

beautiful gold eyes.

Pushed Out, Drawn Up

The ego asks what if, and the brain begins
the chase, letting a quick trickle of light
down a dark path, letting a little light seep in,
    as now,
from the edges of the oak leaves. The leaves

are young, still small as squirrels' ears; they are
tender lime tongues of fresh growth
    pushed out
to the world by sap, pushed out

by the sun; the massive oak manifests
as bifurcations
from trunk to limb and branch to twig; the leaves
    push out

from the burst-open en-
capsulating winter buds,

    push out

to the world, the bright chill air of spring.

But from the sun's point of view it might be
drawn out, not pushed. The oak's sap, after all, is

drawn up the trunk, the limbs, the branches,
the delicate ter-
minating twigs by photosynthesis, cap-
illary action, warmth and evapo-
transpiration.

Which by Definition Is

Cognitive bias can steer one
to confirm a hypothesis under study
or to reject an alternative—either way
a problem. So think about this:

is synchronicity explained best by apophenia,
      which by definition is
the experience of seeing patterns
or connections in random data,

      or by causality,
driven by something
greater than the things
happening, offering truth

to a deeper sense of meaning? Oh, such
a conundrum, such
a contextual problem! Take this

as an example: what if
Émile Deschamps' plum pudding
took off and flew

to Carl Jung's dark window, thumping
to get in? What if

the Pauli Effect was real?

Facts in a Dream

In a night when I dream I can float
down like down from a duck
if I will it, I can, so I float
sometimes from a great height, re-
minding myself, just before
stepping off to begin,

I can do it: and I do it,
settling
with some tension through air
under the force of gravity. How great
be the will
if this floating was true; how

substantial a fact, in fact.
In the dream, it is as though
lines of gravitational force

     just
bend around me, just bend
upon touching my will.

No Chance

The stuff we know now astounds me:
in mice, the Grueneberg ganglion
is a sensory organ for detecting cold
temperatures—it interacts

with a unique type of guanylyl cyclase,
and nanostars can be loaded with
gold cores wrapped in Raman-reporter molecules
surrounded by silica to identify even tiny tumors

and one-two pulses of high-intensity infrared
and ultraviolet laser light can be used to detect
airborne contaminants at a distance, and
human $CD4^+$ helper T cells

are more heterogeneous than we had thought and

it just goes on like this, one
crusty thing after another, there's
no chance, none—
I can't keep up.

I Let Myself Move Down or Up

from where I am to mental and
from mental to mythical,
from mythical to magical,
from magical to archaic—

knowing
each structure of con-
sciousness has its own
positive and negative features, knowing

each one has its own
voids and strengths and,
when called upon, a voice—
not one

calling from the wilderness but one
calling
lantern-like to the beauty of life.

The Durability of Monet

Some things you know are just jaw-
droppingly beautiful or thought
provoking; that's
the nature of the world: we're

hardwired, I think, for beauty. Take,
for example,
the curve of an arm,
the rings from a flat stone skipped

across the slick
surface of a large pond, the first
ring popping just beyond
the pads of yellow water lilies

of the type painted
by Claude Monet—he painted
raw light softened
across far more than hyperspectral colors,

haystacks, bridges, willows, rivers,
cathedrals, train stations, cliffs,
poplars, the Grand Canal, even the Houses
of Parliament and now

successive rings, each
spreading, intercepting, reinforcing and
disrupting, by damping
through time

mathematically the ripples of the others.

Today I Am Rowing

through autumn with easy strokes.
With each pull
eddies curl from the oars and make themselves
visible at the dark

air-water interface.

The eddies sweep the occasional leaf
around and around in brief
little gyres of summer gone.
In this slow rowing

it is so easy to forget

the repetitious days of summer
emerging from the roughshod
exuberance of spring
emerging from the bleak

hard times of winter.

In this slow rowing
I find myself merging
with time and with the beautiful dark
air-water interface.

This Far

We drove
as far into the mountains as we could,
first on a two-lane swooping road,
then cutting off
at a curve to gravel,
then bumping in aspen country,
chuckholes hard enough to scrape
bottom and rattle teeth, all the while

looking up to take in
the sky intensely blue,
and the air was cool and warm
and dry, all at the same time.

Stopped
at last, slamming
car doors behind us to silence.

A flock of magpies
broke the clearing, a quick
flutter of white and black,
leaving, more or less
together, briefly raucous.

The mountains were so big we stumbled
hiking up, over rocks
the size of a fist, a body, a head,
while constantly before us
the real mountains kept rising.

We worked past the last of the aspen,
through Douglas fir, every breath
coming quick and deep,
even when we paused
to make ends meet.

Looking back

down the mountain's rough flank
to the trees below and down
at a red-tail hawk circling above the trees,
it was as though I had become

something like the air
slipping past the hawk's wings:
I had come this far
up the mountain to become something
less than I thought I was.

About the Author

Art Stewart earned his Ph.D. at Michigan State University's Kellogg Biological Station, did postdoctoral research at Oak Ridge National Laboratory (ORNL), then taught and learned stream ecology at the University of Oklahoma before returning to ORNL. At ORNL, he worked as a staff scientist, group leader, senior scientist, and science leader for 17 years. To pursue his interests in improving science education, he then became a science-education project manager for Oak Ridge Associated Universities (ORAU). He lives in Lenoir City, not far from the hubbub of Knoxville, Tennessee, and writes whenever possible. *Elements of Chance* is his sixth collection of science-flavored poems.

Notes

Preface and Acknowledgments, pp. xi

>Combs, A. 2009. *Consciousness Explained Better.* Paragon House, St. Paul, MN. 178 p.

>Combs, A. and M. Holland. 1996. *Synchronicity: Science, Myth, and the Trickster.* Marlowe & Company, New York, NY. 184 p.

>Margulis, L. and D. Sagan. 1997. *Slanted Truths: Essays on Gaia, Symbiosis, and Evolution.* Copernicus, Springer-Verlag, New York, NY. 368 p.

>Rosenblum, B. and F. Kuttner. 2006. *Quantum Enigma. Physics Encounters Consciousness.* Oxford University Press, Oxford, NY. 217 p.

>Satinover, J. 2001. *The Quantum Brain.* John Wiley & Sons, Inc. New York, NY. 276 p.

>Thomas, Lewis. 1974. *The Lives of a Cell: Notes of a Biology Watcher.* Penguin Books, New York, NY. 153 p.

Heisenberg and Spooky Action at a Distance, p. 14

>Oppenheim, J. and S. Wehner. 2010. The uncertainty principle determines the nonlocality of quantum mechanics. *Science* 30(6007):1072-1074. doi: 10.1126/science.1192065

Causalland, p. 19

>Dedicated to Dean Evasius, division director, Division of Graduate Education, National Science Foundation. You go, guy!

Roots of Synchronicity, p. 15

>Combs, A. and M. Holland. 1996. *Synchronicity: Science, Myth, and the Trickster.* Marlowe & Company, New York, NY. 184 pp.

General Relativity, p. 24

> Blanford, R. D. 2015. A century of general relativity: astrophysics and cosmology. *Science* 347(6226):1103-1108.

Edges, p. 50

> http://www.washingtonpost.com/news/speaking-of-science/wp/2015/01/29/why-did-nasa-fire-rockets-at-the-northern-lights/ (accessed January 29, 2015).

Nazca Plate, p. 46

> Grant, R. A., J. P. Raulin, and F. T. Freund. 2015. Changes in animal activity prior to a major (M = 7) earthquake in the Peruvian Andes. *Physics and Chemistry of the Earth* 85-86:69-77.

Well Now, What's This?, p. 47

> Grant, R. A., T. Halliday, W. P. Balderer, F. Leuenerger, M. Newcomer, G. Cyr, and F. T. Freund. 2011. Ground water chemistry changes before major earthquakes and possible effects on animals. *International Journal of Environmental Research and Public Health* 8(6):1936-1956. http://www.cnn.com/2015/04/03/tech/mci-earthquake-animals/

> Heki, K. and Y. Enomoto. 2015. M-w dependence of the preseismic ionospheric electron enhancements. *Journal of Geophysical Research: Space Physics.* 120(8):7006-7020.

> Thériault, R., F. St-Laurent, F. T. Freund, and J. S. Derr. 2014. Prevalence of earthquake lights associated with rift environments. *Seismological Research Letters* 85:159-178.

Siberian Traps, p. 48

> Clarkson, M. O., et al. 2015. Ocean acidification and the Permo-Triassic mass extinction. *Science* 348(6231):229-232.

North, Meet South, p. 49

> Hoorn, C. and S. Flantua. 2015. An early start for the Panama land bridge. *Science* 348(6231):186-187.

The Little Bones, p. 54

> Skinner, M. M., et al. 2015. Human-like hand use in *Australopithecus africanus*. *Science* 347(6220):395-399.

DNA Methylation, p. 55

> Phillips, T. 2008. The role of methylation in gene expression. *Nature Education* 1(1):116.

We're Packed, p. 56

> Finnegan, S., et al. 2015. Paleontological baselines for evaluating extinction risk in the modern oceans. *Science* 348(6234):567-570.

> Hurtley, S. (ed). 2015. Research in *Science* journals. *Science* 348(6234):536-538.

A Weak Whisper, p. 57

> http://www.eurekalert.org/pub_releases/2016-04/uow-rca042116.php

Wheel-Wheel-Horn, p. 58

> Email from Onn Brandman, Stanford University, Department of Biochemistry, January 7, 2015. "Hi Arthur, Neat that you wrote about Rqc2p! Your poem is art so I won't make any direct comments about the work but here are two general comments: 1) Rqc2p still needs ribosomes to make protein. 2) We don't understand why Rqc2 is drives the ribosome to make wheel-horn type additions to stalled proteins, but these additions might be important for cells. Hope this helps. Onn."

> Shen, P. S., J. Park, Y. Qin, X. Li, K. Parsawar, M. H. Larson, J. Cox, Y. Cheng, A. M. Lambowitz, J. S. Weissman, O. Brandman, and A. Frost. 2015. Rqc2p and 60S ribosomal subunits mediate mRNA-independent elongation of nascent chains. *Science* 347(6217):75-78. doi:10.1126/science.1259724

Nanophotonics, p. 68

> Koenderink, A. F., A. Alù, and A. Polman. 2015. Nanophotonics: shrinking light-based technology. *Science* 348(6234):516-521.

Homes, p. 73

    Cho, A. 2015. To catch a wave. *Science* 347(6226):1084-1088.

What's Up, p. 79

    Geisel, T. S. 1947. *McElligot's Pool*. Random House Books, New York, NY. 64 p.

What's in a Word, p. 81

    Cho, A. 2015. Misfire aside, signs of cosmic inflation could come soon. *Science* 347(6222):595-596.

How to Start a Poem, p. 82

    Tomlinson, C. (ed). 1985. *William Carlos Williams: Selected Poems*. New Directions, New York, NY. 302 p.

No Chance, p. 88

    Hurtley, S. (ed.). 2015. Research in *Science* journals. *Science* 347(6220):384-386.

I Let Myself Move Down or Up, p. 89

    Combs, A. 2009. *Consciousness Explained Better*. Paragon House, St. Paul, MN. 178. p.

www.ingramcontent.com/pod-product-compliance
Lightning Source LLC
Chambersburg PA
CBHW071232090426
42736CB00014B/3058